VAR ROONEY: THE WAGATHA CHRISTIE TRIAL

by Liv Hennessy

SAMUEL FRENCH

FOR AMATEUR PRODUCTION ENQUIRIES

UNITED KINGDOM AND WORLD
EXCLUDING NORTH AMERICA
licensing@concordtheatricals.co.uk
020-7054-7298

Each title is subject to availability from Concord Theatricals,
depending upon country of performance.

USE OF COPYRIGHTED MUSIC

USE OF COPYRIGHTED THIRD-PARTY MATERIALS

IMPORTANT BILLING AND CREDIT REQUIREMENTS

Vardy V Rooney: The Wagatha Christie Trial was commissioned and originally produced by Eleanor Lloyd Productions and Eilene Davidson Productions. The production was first performed at the Wyndham's Theatre in the West End from 15 November 2022 for seven performances only, followed by a transfer to the Ambassadors Theatre in the West End from 6 April 2023 before a UK and Ireland tour. The casts were as follows:

Wyndham's Theatre Cast (in order of appearance)

COLEEN ROONEY	Laura Dos Santos
PUNDIT 1 (JEFF)/JAMIE VARDY/WAYNE ROONEY	Nathan McMullen
PUNDIT 2 (JEM)/HARPREET ROBERTSON/CAROLINE WATT	Sharan Phull
REBEKAH VARDY	Lucy May Barker
HUGH TOMLINSON QC	Jonnie Broadbent
DAVID SHERBORNE	Tom Turner
MRS JUSTICE STEYN	Charlotte Randle

Ambassadors Theatre Cast (in order of appearance)

COLEEN ROONEY	Laura Dos Santos
PUNDIT 1 (JEFF)/JAMIE VARDY/WAYNE ROONEY	Nathan McMullen
PUNDIT 2 (JEM)/HARPREET ROBERTSON/CAROLINE WATT	Halema Hussain
REBEKAH VARDY	Lucy May Barker
HUGH TOMLINSON QC	Jonnie Broadbent
DAVID SHERBORNE	Tom Turner
MRS JUSTICE STEYN	Verna Vyas
UNDERSTUDIES	Ceili O'Connor, Tom Sullivan

CREATIVE TEAM

ADAPTOR	Liv Hennessy
DIRECTOR	Lisa Spirling
SET AND COSTUME DESIGNER	Polly Sullivan
LIGHTING DESIGNER (WYNDHAM'S THEATRE)	Ben Bull
LIGHTING DESIGNER (AMBASSADORS THEATRE)	Johanna Town
COMPOSER AND SOUND DESIGNER	Richard Hammarton
CASTING DIRECTOR	Naomi Downham
COSTUME SUPERVISOR	Hugo Aguirre
ASSISTANT DIRECTOR	Lizzie Manwaring
DRAMATURG	Sarah Dickenson
MOVEMENT CONSULTANT	Mateus Daniel

CHARACTERS

COLEEN ROONEY

PUNDIT 1 – called **JEFF** – also **JAMIE VARDY/WAYNE ROONEY**

PUNDIT 2 – called **JEM** – also **HARPREET ROBERTSON/CAROLINE WATT**

REBEKAH VARDY

HUGH TOMLINSON QC

DAVID SHERBORNE

MRS JUSTICE STEYN

AUTHOR'S NOTES

Notes on the text

"..." signifies a break in the verbatim text, NOT a pause.

"[...]" signifies a spoken "dot dot dot".

"–" signifies an interruption, by a character's own thoughts or by each other.

Text in [brackets] is for clarity, and should be spoken as part of the text.

Vardy v Rooney: The Wagatha Christie Trial was commissioned by Eleanor Lloyd Productions and Eilene Davidson Productions.

ELEANOR LLOYD
PRODUCTIONS

EILENE DAVIDSON
PRODUCTIONS

1.

(Lights up on a court room.)

(We're with **COLEEN ROONEY** *– holding a notepad and pen.)*

COLEEN. For a few years now, someone who I trusted to follow me on my personal Instagram account has been consistently informing *The Sun* newspaper of my private posts and stories. There has been so much information given to them about me, my friends and my family – all without my permission or knowledge.

After a long time of trying to figure out who it could be, for various reasons, I had a suspicion. To try and prove this, I came up with an idea. I blocked everyone from viewing my Instagram stories except ONE account. (Those on my private account must have been wondering why I haven't had stories on there for a while.)

Over the past five months, I have posted a series of false stories to see if they made their way into *The Sun* newspaper. And you know what, they did! The story about gender selection in Mexico, the story about returning to TV and then the latest story about the basement flooding in my new house.

It's been tough keeping it to myself and not making any comment at all, especially when the stories have been leaked, however I had to. Now I know for certain which account/individual it's come from.

I have saved and screenshotted all the original stories which clearly show just one person has viewed them.

It's [..........] Rebekah Vardy's account.

(**COLEEN** *freezes and we're with* **PUNDIT 1** *&* **PUNDIT 2**.)

PUNDIT 1. Bold play there from Rooney in October 2019.

PUNDIT 2. Bold is the word, Jeff, because that social media post has landed her here today – at the High Court in London on 20th May 2022 – over *three years later*.

PUNDIT 1. That's right. And we're with you, court-side, about to kick off one of the most highly anticipated libel cases of all time.

PUNDIT 2. It's definitely been a lengthy preparation period for both teams, hasn't it Jeff, but they made it. This is Rebekah Vardy versus Coleen Rooney, in their own words.

PUNDIT 1. Yep, every word you hear in this court is *exactly* what was recorded across seven days of court transcripts.

PUNDIT 2. Well, not *every* word. We weren't in court, obviously.

PUNDIT 1. No, we weren't. And, as we all know, it took seven days to lay out the evidence, and then two months for the Judge to deliver her verdict –

PUNDIT 2. And we haven't got time for that.

PUNDIT 1. No. But you're here in *our* theatre of dreams. So what you're about to see is ninety minutes of match highlights.

PUNDIT 2. Don't worry, we'll step in when it all gets a bit technical.

PUNDIT 1. That's right, because libel's played a bit differently in the UK, isn't it Jem?

PUNDIT 2. You're bang on, Jeff. Here, in a British court, the burden of proof rests on the publisher. And in this match, that's Coleen Rooney and her social media post.

PUNDIT 1. So whether she likes it or not, she's going to have to go on the attack?

PUNDIT 2. Absolutely. Coleen Rooney has to *prove* that Rebekah Vardy was leaking stories about her, or she loses the case.

PUNDIT 1. Ahhh, but let's not forget, if Coleen can't win this case on the truth defence – which I'm pretty sure she will –

PUNDIT 2. Let's see about that –

PUNDIT 1. – then she *can* win by arguing that posting it was in the public interest.

PUNDIT 2. But, Jeff, surely there's a difference between what's in the public interest, and what interests the public.

PUNDIT 1. Jem, this is probably a good time to say – we're not legal experts.

PUNDIT 2. No.

PUNDIT 1. And we should also add – for broadcast reasons – how we, the pundits, perceive the events of this trial might not necessarily be accepted by Coleen Rooney or Rebekah Vardy.

PUNDIT 2. Because it's not always a beautiful game. There's friendships, betrayal, marriages on the brink –

PUNDIT 1. Villains, ghosts, wigs –

PUNDIT 2. And two women who happen to be married to footballers.

(*The* **PUNDITS** *touch earpieces.*)

PUNDIT 1. And – yep – we've just been told we're seconds away from kick off.

PUNDIT 2. The stadium's filled, the warm-up is complete –

PUNDIT 1. In the words of Norwich City's major shareholder, Delia Smith – "let's be having ya" –

PUNDIT 2. Where are ya, come ooooon.

> *(The court takes shape around them. We're on the Judge and the barristers, all completely frozen.* **PUNDIT 2** *moves towards* **MR TOMLINSON**.*)*

In the attacking midfield, we've got Rebekah Vardy, with her barrister Mr Tomlinson.

> *(***PUNDIT 1** *moves towards* **MR SHERBORNE**.*)*

PUNDIT 1. And playing in defence, we have Coleen Rooney, and her barrister Mr Sherborne.

PUNDIT 2. But, most importantly, the referee for tonight's title clash – our judge, Mrs Justice Steyn.

PUNDIT 1. Before we start, Jem, we should mention…. we might be subbing in for some other key players when needed.

PUNDIT 2. But for now, we are your pundits.

PUNDIT 1. Humble observers to the beautiful game. Just like you.

> *(The* **PUNDITS** *retreat.)*

> *(***STEYN** *blows a whistle and the game begins.)*

TOMLINSON. My Lady, with the court's permission, I'll call Mrs Vardy.

(**REBEKAH VARDY** *takes the stand. She puts her hand on something and takes a sharp intake of breath, and –.*)

(*The* **PUNDITS** *gather.*)

PUNDIT 2. Here, the court docs simply say that Rebekah Vardy is 'sworn in'.

PUNDIT 1. We're not allowed to know if this was on a holy book, or an atheist reading –

PUNDIT 2. But the sentiment is the same. Rebekah Vardy has to tell the truth.

(*The* **PUNDITS** *retreat.*)

TOMLINSON. First of all, can you give the court your full name.

REBEKAH. Yes, it is Rebekah Vardy.

TOMLINSON. … You should have a trial bundle which consists of bundles A to F … I try to remember to say to all witnesses and then forget – you have got quite a soft voice. The most important person in the court is the Judge… so it is important that the Judge hears rather than the rest of us.

REBEKAH. OK.

(**MR TOMLINSON** *sits*. **MR SHERBORNE** *stands.*)

SHERBORNE. Mrs Vardy, let's see if we can start by agreeing on a few things. You would agree, wouldn't you… to secretly pass on somebody else's information that they didn't want shared with the outside world is wrong, isn't it?

REBEKAH. Yes, my Lady…

SHERBORNE. You'd hate to be called a leak, wouldn't you?

REBEKAH. I have been called a leak. It's not nice...

SHERBORNE. Mrs Vardy... would you say you respect people's privacy?

REBEKAH. Yes, I do.

SHERBORNE. Let's test that. ... I'm going to take you to an... article that we [have] in Bundle D. ... This is an interview you gave to Jane Atkinson, who is a journalist... at *The News of the World*... in March 2004.... about having had sex with Peter Andre... do you know roughly what the circulation was of the News of the World in 2004?

REBEKAH. No, I don't.

SHERBORNE. Let me help you. It was probably about four million people... the highest circulating newspaper at that time... the article which has a picture of you – that is you, isn't it? – on the left hand side?

REBEKAH. That is, yeah.

SHERBORNE. And then you have Mr Andre on the right-hand side, entitled: "Peter's hung like a small chipolata, shaved, slobbery, lasts five minutes then falls asleep... Stunning Rebekah Nicholson reckons she has the perfect title for pop poser Peter Andre's performance with her in bed: I've got a chipolata, get me out of here". Your words, Mrs Vardy?

REBEKAH. Yes, my Lady. Can I give a bit of history on that one please?

SHERBORNE. I'll give you the opportunity to say what I expect you're going to say, Mrs Vardy, but perhaps we can just deal with whether these are your words.

REBEKAH. ... They are the words I'm reading, yes.

SHERBORNE. ... Let me ask you this, Mrs Vardy, do you think it was respectful of Mr Andre's right not to share this information with the world?

REBEKAH. My Lady, I was forced into a situation by my ex-husband to do this story. This is something I deeply regret and something that is very much part of my past. It's not nice to read, and I have dealt with this and understand why this is being used, because to me this is mud-slinging and I was always threatened with mud-slinging by Mrs Rooney's team.

SHERBORNE. Did you ask Mr Andre's permission first?

REBEKAH. Again, I was forced into doing something that I didn't want to do.

SHERBORNE. That's not an answer to the question, Mrs Vardy. Did you or did you not ask Mr Andre's permission first?

REBEKAH. Of course not.

SHERBORNE. ... To be fair to you, I should ask, did you feel particularly strongly about the size of his manhood that it should be made public?

REBEKAH. Again, it was something I was forced to say.

SHERBORNE. Turning to... D1 at page 1822 ...the WhatsApp exchanges [where] you authorised or approved the provision of information to the press by Ms Watt. This is an exchange between you and Caroline Watt, is that right? ... You are Bex and she is Caroline, obviously.

REBEKAH. I am.

SHERBORNE. We know this is about someone called Riyad Mahrez, because he's named in your WhatsApp exchange... just so we are clear, [Mahrez] was a colleague of your husband Jamie at Leicester City football club, wasn't he?

REBEKAH. He was at the time, yes.

SHERBORNE. Let's see what you say –

REBEKAH. "Mahrez not turned up to training again... Lads are fuming" –

SHERBORNE. ...to which Caroline replies –

*(The **PUNDITS** gather.)*

PUNDIT 2. I think now is a good time to explain – there's actually somebody not on the field today who really should be. Caroline Watt.

PUNDIT 1. Rebekah's former friend and agent, crucially missing from everyone's starting eleven. Sadly, Caroline Watt withdrew her statement and refused to come to court.

PUNDIT 2. She didn't *refuse,* Jeff. She was excused, on medical grounds.

PUNDIT 1. Now, you may or may not recall, that some of Rebekah's messages mysteriously vanished.

PUNDIT 2. That was actually due to a technical error during download.

PUNDIT 1. And then Caroline's phone famously ended up in the North Sea...

PUNDIT 2. She has a weakness in her hand.

PUNDIT 1. So that basically means that we don't have any WhatsApp media files – voicenotes, pictures, videos – across the period of interest, i.e. when Coleen was uploading fake posts. It means this court is missing *crucial* evidence.

PUNDIT 2. Look, these things happen in a game like this.

PUNDIT 1. But we've got *some* messages. Because Coleen's legal team did a little bit of magic down the opposition wing – he requested Rebekah's WhatsApp messages from months *before* the period of Coleen's posts. A tactic she wasn't expecting.

PUNDIT 2. I mean, nobody comes out well from that, do they? Your private messages being read out to a public audience. It's everyone's worst nightmare.

PUNDIT 1. I mean, if mine were to be... but, back to court, the lads were fuming.

*(The **PUNDITS** retreat.)*

REBEKAH. "Mahrez not turned up to training again... Lads are fuming"–

SHERBORNE. ...to which Caroline replies –

*(A pause... and **PUNDIT 2** becomes **CAROLINE**.)*

CAROLINE. "Really? Why don't you tell Rob Dorsett?"

SHERBORNE. ... [He's] the Sky Sports reporter... and you say –

REBEKAH. "Just don't want it coming back on me".

CAROLINE. "I can tell someone'"

REBEKAH. "Yeah do it'"

CAROLINE. "Okay" ...

SHERBORNE. ... You didn't want it coming back on you? ... You see, once you knew that Ms Watt would do the dirty for you, you were happy for the information to be leaked, weren't you?

REBEKAH. ... As it reads there, it doesn't read well, but it was because it would reflect badly if there was any gossip that had directly come from me.

SHERBORNE. ... Can we turn to the next example... page 1831 ... The next example refers to someone called 'Mrs F' in order to protect her identity... to give this context, Mrs F is a well known celebrity, right?

REBEKAH. That's correct, yes,

SHERBORNE. Mr H is her estranged husband... they were separated because of marital difficulties... and Mr G is a well known footballer. Without giving too much information away... there were pictures of [Mrs F] on a beach, dancing around... wearing relatively little clothing... let's read together what you said to Caroline Watt –

REBEKAH. "[Oh my god] have you seen how badly Mrs F is behaving".

SHERBORNE. ... And she says –

CAROLINE. "I haven't seen it, I'll look –"

SHERBORNE. And you say –

REBEKAH. "Leak the story about her shagging Mr G behind Mr H's back".

CAROLINE. "I tried before but *The Sun* already knew about it. And couldn't prove it as usual".

SHERBORNE. To which you respond –

REBEKAH. "Ugh" –

SHERBORNE. ... What you say is "Ugh", you're annoyed that you can't leak it, aren't you?

REBEKAH. It's more like an ugh, not an uh...

SHERBORNE. You're annoyed, aren't you? ...

REBEKAH. No... I was actually just joking about that one.

SHERBORNE. You were just joking?

REBEKAH. Yes, I was.

SHERBORNE. ... You [use] the word leak, don't you?

REBEKAH. I did use the word leak but that's not what I meant.

SHERBORNE. ... Oh I see. You don't know what the word leak means then?

REBEKAH. Well, there are two meanings, but that's not what I meant by the word 'leak'.

SHERBORNE. ... You say this is a joke... is that your evidence to the court?

REBEKAH. Ms Watt and myself have been friends for a very long time. Our WhatsApps were sometimes outrageous, sometimes totally inappropriate... and yes, they don't read very well. But there's always explanations for them.

SHERBORNE. ... Let's turn to the next example. Danny Drinkwater... page 1855 ... he was a professional footballer, yes?

REBEKAH. Yes, that's correct.

SHERBORNE. You message Caroline Watt again, you initiate a message at eight fifty nine in the evening of 8th April of 2019. And this is what you say –

REBEKAH. "Story [...]" –

SHERBORNE. – We have that convention of the "[...]" when you are about to announce something –

REBEKAH. "[...] Danny Drinkwater arrested".

SHERBORNE. And she asks you –

CAROLINE. "For what".

REBEKAH. "Crashed his car drunk with two girls in it... both in hospital, one with broken ribs" –

SHERBORNE. And then you say –

REBEKAH. "I want paying for this"

SHERBORNE. Is this another joke?

REBEKAH. ... No, it's absolutely not a joke.

SHERBORNE. ... So you meant it when you said "I want paying for this".

REBEKAH. No, I meant in the context that – ... I'm deeply affected by drink driving, my ex-husband killed two people during our marriage and it was something that I felt was outrageous, and at the time I didn't care whether the information came out or not. It was something that rightly should – someone should have to... they were going to get away with it.

SHERBORNE. ... Oh, I see... And then [Caroline] says –

CAROLINE. "... News are already on it... someone leaked it from the police station" –

REBEKAH. "Fuck somebody already tipped it"

SHERBORNE. ... You're angry. You're not angry because this story about someone who's done something awful is out, because it's coming out anyway. What you are angry about is that you're not going to get your money.

REBEKAH. No, that's not true...

SHERBORNE. You're angry, aren't you?

REBEKAH. No.

SHERBORNE. ... Let's just see what you say eight seconds later –

REBEKAH. "I'm fuming I didn't give it you earlier" ...

SHERBORNE. And Caroline Watt knows why you're fuming doesn't she, because she says –

CAROLINE. "Me too that would have been a fortune" ...

REBEKAH. That's correct, but with laughing faces... that was Caroline's sense of humour –

SHERBORNE. ... I see, so it's another joke is it? ... Can you turn, please, to page 273. Do you see that is your witness statement... and this is your signature here, isn't it?

REBEKAH. That's correct, yes.

SHERBORNE. And you know the consequences of getting it wrong, don't you, of saying something that's not true in there?

REBEKAH. Well, something that might not be right, yes.

SHERBORNE. Something that might not be right? What do you mean by that?

REBEKAH. Well, it's just... I'm just elaborating on what you were saying.

SHERBORNE. You read this statement very carefully, didn't you? Because if it said something you didn't know to be true, you know the consequences, don't you?

REBEKAH. Yes.

> *(The **PUNDITS** gather.)*

PUNDIT 1. He's lined her up – and once he's through on goal...

> *(The **PUNDITS** retreat.)*

SHERBORNE. ... [This is] on page 266 [of] your witness statement.

REBEKAH. ... "I have sometimes been caught up in the heat of the moment during conversations with Caroline where I have talked about leaks and payment... but these conversations were *never* serious and Caroline would have understood that. I have *never* been paid for private information about anyone apart from myself or my family".

SHERBORNE. Mrs Vardy, do you still stand by that evidence? ... Yes or no please, Mrs Vardy.

REBEKAH. Yes, apart from the Danny Drinkwater one.

SHERBORNE. Oh I see, so there is an exception... what this shows, Mrs Vardy, is you are prepared to lie under oath, aren't you?

*(The **PUNDITS** gather.)*

PUNDIT 1. Back of the net.

PUNDIT 2. OK, fine. But it's still early days. And to be clear, Rebekah isn't on trial over Danny Drinkwater or Peter Andre. She's here because of Coleen.

PUNDIT 1. Yeah, we should probably get to that. The moment when Coleen and Rebekah come face to face. It's England versus Wales.

PUNDIT 2. Quite literally. This is the Euros 2016 football match, when Jamie Vardy and Wayne Rooney both played in Roy Hodgson's England squad. Vardy even got the equaliser.

PUNDIT 1. But Rebekah was busy too. She got a column in *The Sun* during the Euros.

*(The **PUNDITS** retreat.)*

SHERBORNE. … Can we turn to page 2273. 12 June 2016. And this is the Euro diary, it's your column in *The Sun*?

REBEKAH. Yes that's right.

SHERBORNE. Ms Watt has arranged for you to have a column [during the tournament] … she has done well, hasn't she?

REBEKAH. I suppose you could call it that. I don't know.

SHERBORNE. This is you getting a chance to promote yourself?

REBEKAH. No, this is an opportunity for me to be able to earn my own money, and I never wanted to rely on my husband. I wanted to earn my own money and there was opportunities that arose and both Jamie and I discussed it, and there was no problem with doing that.

SHERBORNE. … [In your column], we have a photograph… 'Rebekah Vardy, left. Coleen Rooney, right', and [you've written] –

REBEKAH. "I was sitting just behind Coleen Rooney watching the game and we had a chat before it started".

SHERBORNE. ... Mrs Vardy, you wanted to put in your diary piece that you were sitting just behind Coleen Rooney watching the game [because] that boosts your public profile?

REBEKAH. No that's just ridiculous.

SHERBORNE. ... What you don't say, Mrs Vardy, is that the reason you were sitting behind Mrs Rooney is because you deliberately went and sat there even though they weren't your seats.

REBEKAH. That's not true at all.

SHERBORNE. You know what [Mrs Robertson, the FA family liaison] says, don't you? ... Mrs Vardy, you are pulling a face?

REBEKAH. Because it's Mrs Robertson... If I may, [she] took an instant dislike to me.

SHERBORNE. We will come back to that... Mrs Robertson [said] that you knew exactly where the cameras would be and that's why you and your party sat behind Mrs Rooney, and when she asked you to move, she was told to fuck off?

REBEKAH. I can't recall ever anyone saying that, no.

SHERBORNE. When you say you can't recall, do you mean it didn't happen?

REBEKAH. It means I can't recall. 2016 is a long time ago.

SHERBORNE. ... Somebody telling a Football Association liaison ticket officer... to fuck off... that's something you'd remember if it happened, wouldn't you?

REBEKAH. ... The stadium was very loud.

SHERBORNE. Whatever happened, Mrs Vardy, you were going to sit in those seats, weren't you? [Because] if you sit behind Mrs Rooney you will definitely get good photo coverage.

REBEKAH. No that's not true at all... and I find it quite interesting... because I think it's nonsense. Absolute nonsense.

SHERBORNE. ... One of you is not telling the truth, isn't that correct?

REBEKAH. Or maybe Mrs Robertson has completely forgotten, I mean it was 2016.

SHERBORNE. So she's lying, is she?

REBEKAH. I think she is – has either got confused or it's what she's been told to say.

SHERBORNE. What she's been told to say? Who has she been told to say this by?

REBEKAH. I don't know.

SHERBORNE. ... Let me set the scene Mrs Vardy... 2018 World Cup Russia. You're in St Petersburg, yes?

REBEKAH. Yes.

SHERBORNE. A number of the partners of players went out for a meal in a restaurant the night before – I think it was the Belgian game in the first round?

REBEKAH. Yes.

SHERBORNE. And that dinner gets reported the next day, 'World Cup 2018. England Wags including Rebekah Vardy look glamorous as they head out for dinner' ... And there's a line-up we see with the players who are related to the various girlfriends or partners?

REBEKAH. ... Yes, that's correct.

SHERBORNE. ... 5145 ...you will see that is [Harpreet Robertson's] statement, and [she says] –

(**PUNDIT 2** *becomes* **HARPREET ROBERTSON.**)

MRS ROBERTSON. "I recall a photograph which was published in the press with Becky and most of the other Wags of the England team during the 2018 World Cup lined up outside a restaurant they had attended. [I recall being told that] Becky had not asked some of the older ladies present at the hotel to attend the dinner she had arranged... I remember several ladies in the family hotel, players, sisters and mothers, who were upset they had not been invited to the dinner but the photograph set-up seemed to explain why, as a Wag shot was the objective of the night'.

REBEKAH. No that's not true. There was a group WhatsApp chat... and everyone just wanted it to be just the girls.

SHERBORNE. It's a photograph of young attractive women, let's be honest, Mrs Vardy, so no one who was old was going to be asked, were they?

REBEKAH. That's not how it went at all, no.

SHERBORNE. ... Let's look at what was happening behind the scenes... you see, we have the conversation between you and Ms Watt on page 1827 ... you say this –

REBEKAH. "We may walk to restaurant from hotel now so might be a good pic of us walking down. It's about ten to fifteen minutes away".

CAROLINE. "OK, hopefully he catches you all. Don't forget to take a group shot at the table"

REBEKAH. ... "Yeah will do but someone will put it online before they can use it".

SHERBORNE. ... And then –

REBEKAH. "Fuck I made everyone go outside for a pic and the pap was there... [It] looks like I've tipped him off now".

SHERBORNE. The pap is standing there and it looks like you've tipped him off, and it has this effect, which is exactly what you worry about –

REBEKAH. "[The] girls have asked me to put it on insta so quick get them out... they want me to put it up before the pap puts his in!"

SHERBORNE. What you are worried about there [is that] all the financial benefit of that will disappear the minute someone at the table puts their own photograph up online. That's right, isn't it? The exclusive has gone.

REBEKAH. No that's not true...

SHERBORNE. And then you say –

REBEKAH. "I've bought about ten mins".

SHERBORNE. You've bought the photographer ten minutes to get it online so that the exclusive is not thwarted by the girls putting their Instagram photo up, true or false?

REBEKAH. While it reads like that, I don't recall it like that. And if I'm completely honest, my Lady, I had been drinking quite a bit that day.

SHERBORNE. This is the first time in this courtroom you have ever said that somehow your recollection of this is because you may have drunk too much. That's a lie, isn't it?

REBEKAH. ... No, it's not... If I'm honest, I can't remember this at all.

SHERBORNE. Well I would much rather you're honest because you are sitting in a witness box under oath... can I then ask you to focus for a moment on Mrs Rooney. As you say in your statement you asked to be one of the followers on her private Instagram, didn't you?

REBEKAH. Yes.

SHERBORNE. That was when? I think you say January 2017?

REBEKAH. Approximately 2017. January. Yes.

SHERBORNE. Can I take you to bundle D1. This is the car crash post... it was on Mrs Rooney's private Instagram account –

COLEEN. ... 'RIP Half a Honda' –

SHERBORNE. – and then you can see [a picture of] the side of the car sort of caved in... now, can you turn back to the WhatsApp exchanges between you and Ms Watt which is more than twenty four hours after the car crash post... that post would have expired... so let's look at what she says –

CAROLINE. "... Am I imagining this or did you say yesterday that Coleen had crashed her Honda?".

SHERBORNE. And you say –

REBEKAH. "She deffo has. Go to Instagram".

SHERBORNE. ... Caroline Watt is going into Mrs Rooney's private Instagram account through using your account... you're actually directing her to do so, aren't you?

REBEKAH. Yes, on that occasion. I didn't even think about it.

SHERBORNE. ... Caroline says –

CAROLINE. "I would have tried to have done a story on Coleen but the evidence has been deleted" –

SHERBORNE. That's the Instagram story, isn't it?

REBEKAH. I'm not sure what she was referring to here.

SHERBORNE. ... Two pages on –

CAROLINE. ... "[Andy Halls at *The Sun*] is trying to do a story on Coleen crashing her car but her PR won't even reply".

SHERBORNE. You don't say to her... what do you mean Caroline? Why is Andy Halls trying to do a story? No. You laugh.

REBEKAH. "Haha, she defo did it".

SHERBORNE. ... Mrs Vardy, you confirmed to *The Sun* through Caroline Watt that Mrs Rooney had crashed her car. But she hadn't, had she?

REBEKAH. Well, I don't know whether she had actually crashed her car.

SHERBORNE. ... If you go to 531 in the bundle, you will see, top right hand... *The Sun*, 25th January 2019 ...it is the car crash article... 'Coleen Rooney narrowly avoids injury in car crash and wrecks 4x4 just weeks after Wayne's arrest for public intoxication in Washington' ... Do you see that?

REBEKAH. Yes.

SHERBORNE. ... 'A source told *The Sun*... "The motor was a mess. One side of the car was completely caved in...it looked like a total write-off'. It doesn't say Rest in Peace but it might as well have done. Yes, Mrs Vardy?

REBEKAH. Yes.

SHERBORNE. ... This is Mrs Rooney's reaction to this. She puts up on a private account –

COLEEN. "Someone on here is selling stories again to this scum of a paper".

SHERBORNE. I am not going to go into her views about *The Sun*, they are probably very similar to most people in Liverpool... page 1952 ... On public twitter, [Mrs Rooney] says –

COLEEN. "Thanks for the messages asking if I'm okay. The car crash story was completely wrong. I wasn't involved in a crash. The car was damaged by another car. Someone on my private Instagram seen the picture and is telling or selling stories to a certain newspaper... It's happened several times now over the past couple of years... it's sad to think someone, who I have accepted to follow me, is betraying [me] for either money or to keep a relationship with the press".

SHERBORNE. Correct, wasn't she?

REBEKAH. I don't know.

SHERBORNE. You don't know. Even though you're the person who passed on the information to *The Sun*?

REBEKAH. *The Sun* already had the information.

SHERBORNE. ... 1839 ... this is you speaking to Caroline Watt [after Coleen's public warning]. You message her.

REBEKAH. "U seen Coleen's twitter?"

CAROLINE. "No?"

SHERBORNE. ... Then Caroline says –

CAROLINE. "Just looked. Such a victim. Poor Coleen".

SHERBORNE. And then two laughing emojis. She obviously finds this very funny, doesn't she?

REBEKAH. I don't know whether they are laughing or crying.

SHERBORNE. OK ... and then these words from Caroline –

CAROLINE. "And it wasn't someone she trusted... it was me."

(The **PUNDITS** *gather.)*

PUNDIT 1. Ooooh. Yeah. They've let one in there.

PUNDIT 2. OK – not – *great.*

PUNDIT 1. Let's take a look at that again –

> (*Live action replay. We're on* **CAROLINE** *again –.*)

CAROLINE. "And it wasn't someone she trusted... it was me."

> (*The* **PUNDITS** *retreat.*)

SHERBORNE. She's admitting there, isn't she, what you knew already which is that she is the one who passed the story on to *The Sun*?

REBEKAH. That seems to be what she's saying but I'm just looking at the times. At 18.47 I'm bathing my children. There's no response from me.

SHERBORNE. ... After you've done the bathing of your children why didn't you come back and say, I've just read what you've written. I can't believe it?

REBEKAH. Because if I may, my Lady, I have seen the conversation that follows and without wanting to make fun of anyone it was actually *Dancing on Ice*, and Gemma Collins face planting on the ice was the next message.

SHERBORNE. Let's go back over the other posts from [Coleen's] private Instagram account... let's start with the 'marriage article' ...page 230.

REBEKAH. I have an [article] that says 'Wayne Rooney fears his marriage is over –'

SHERBORNE. ... Let's read it together. It is a nasty story about Mrs Rooney and her husband... and then it says this: [Coleen] uploaded two poignant photos of [her sons] on her Instagram account and wrote –

COLEEN. "No matter where I am they always follow me, and I hope that lasts for ever".

REBEKAH. Yeah, that's nice.

SHERBORNE. ... Let's read it together: 'on Coleen's Instagram account... it shows Wayne cuddled up for the family snap. It's confirmation that pregnant Coleen has finally forgiven her husband' ... So *The Sun* was given either the photograph, the post itself of her children on her private Instagram account or was told about the contents... do you agree?

REBEKAH. I can't comment.

SHERBORNE. ... You see, Mrs Vardy, just listen to my question. That article refers explicitly to a post on Mrs Rooney's Instagram account. And I put it to you that that came from you, through Ms Watt, to [*The Sun*]?

REBEKAH. No, that's not true.

SHERBORNE. True or not true.

REBEKAH. No. Absolutely not.

SHERBORNE. You see, the shame is, isn't it, Mrs Vardy, that [Caroline Watt's phone is] lying at the bottom of the sea, in Davy Jones's locker.

REBEKAH. Who is Davy Jones?

STEYN. It just means at the bottom of the sea.

SHERBORNE. ... [*The Sun* journalists were] not prepared to come to court and say neither you nor Ms Watt were the source, even though you had waived protection... it is on that basis that you ditched Ms Watt, isn't it?

REBEKAH. I don't understand the question.

*(The **PUNDITS** gather.)*

PUNDIT 1. So Sherborne's mentioned waiving protection there.

PUNDIT 2. That's right, Jeff. Source protection. It's legislation that means journalists don't have to reveal the identity of an anonymous source. And Rebekah's waived her right to it – because she has nothing to hide. She wanted to make sure that journalists could legally come forward and prove her innocence.

PUNDIT 1. Which would have probably worked if any journalists had come forward –

PUNDIT 2. Well, you know, there's an ethical question over whether courts should even *allow* journalists to waive source protection –

PUNDIT 1. Either way, the point Sherborne's making is that – no journalists coming to court to say that Caroline and Rebekah *weren't* the source of their articles – looked quite bad. And because Rebekah knew how bad it looked, she shifted tactics. She changed her statement and started to blame her friend and agent, Caroline Watt.

PUNDIT 2. Just to clarify for broadcast there, Jeff, Rebekah has always said that *she herself* is innocent. But in her changed witness statement, she added that she can't speak for Caroline Watt's innocence. Rebekah said that she simply doesn't know.

PUNDIT 1. But back to the game. Rebekah didn't understand the question.

*(The **PUNDITS** retreat.)*

REBEKAH. I don't understand the question.

SHERBORNE. So you say. Let's move on... you see, Mrs Rooney was extremely upset about this... she puts up on her private Instagram account part of that article... another warning shot... and she says...

COLEEN. "The grass strikes again" –

SHERBORNE. This is what she calls the person –

COLEEN. "I put that picture up wondering if it would appear in that horrible newspaper. You're accepted as one of my friends... if you really needed the money that bad you could have always asked instead of being SLY".

SHERBORNE. ... So here she is again putting up a warning to everyone... and then... she puts this up [on her Instagram] –

COLEEN. "Sorry, me again. It's not that picture of me and the kids that's been sold as that picture is on my Twitter and public Instagram. It's the comment that there was a picture of Wayne and the kids. They can't print the picture as it's on my private account... but they have been told it's on there. Not that it's a bad thing them knowing. It's just the fact that someone is telling them what I'm putting up. It's the fourth thing in recent weeks I've noticed".

SHERBORNE. She's clearly upset, isn't she?

REBEKAH. ... She's clearly very upset, yes.

COLEEN. ... "I'm fine thanks to the people asking. Just disappointed I put my trust in people and that's what they do. Well I can honestly say I've been through my followers and I can't pinpoint anyone, so either you're hiding it very well or what I'm hoping someone has lost their phone with their Instagram account on and it's some random person selling it. No point me getting a new account because I'm just going to accept the same people. Rant over. I'm now going to watch Harry Styles in concert. Go and tell the paper that".

SHERBORNE. You see she's trying to find out who it is, isn't she... and you saw that article and that post... and this is how you write to her... it's page 1886 ...at the top...

REBEKAH. "OMG what the fuck is wrong with people? Why have they taken that one of you and the kids and not of Wayne in bed? That would have been an even better story in their minds. Dickheads. Hope you're OK".

SHERBORNE. ... You knew perfectly well, from the training you have working with Ms Watt in passing stories to *The Sun* that they couldn't actually use a photograph [if it's on a private Instagram] … [So] it takes a couple of days for Mrs Rooney to respond. She says –

COLEEN. "Sorry love just getting back to everyone. Been up the wall since I got back off holiday. It was the picture of Wayne and the kids they gave to *The Sun*. However they can't print it so they've just written about it".

REBEKAH. "That's so bad and *The Sun* of all people as well. Have you been through all your followers? No one with any celeb mag links? What about being hacked? I'd be chomping if it was me. Not on at all".

SHERBORNE.   … That's totally disingenuous, isn't it, Mrs Vardy?

REBEKAH. No.

SHERBORNE. You knew perfectly well that you have been responsible, through Ms Watt, [of] passing information to *The Sun*.

REBEKAH. No.

SHERBORNE. … After the car crash post and the warning that Mrs Rooney puts out, she blocks you, doesn't she?

REBEKAH. Yes.

SHERBORNE. … Because she suspects that you are the person responsible, correct?

REBEKAH. From Mrs Rooney's witness statement that is correct, but wrongly so.

SHERBORNE. … Let's look at page 1845 … 6th February… You're trying to work out what you should do about the fact that Mrs Rooney has [just] unfollowed you… you say [to Ms Watt] …

REBEKAH. "I never usually message her and say hi… maybe I should say something about Rosie?"

SHERBORNE. Who's Rosie, Mrs Vardy?

REBEKAH. Coleen's deceased sister.

SHERBORNE. ... So you were going to use the excuse of Coleen's deceased sister to message her... because it was the anniversary of her passing.

REBEKAH. I can't recall properly.

SHERBORNE. I see... And then Caroline comes up with [this] –

CAROLINE. "Just say you did *Loose Women* today and the booker was asking about her and said please let her know we would love her on if she would consider it... [Say] I thought I had better pass it on just in case".

SHERBORNE. Slightly nicer peg than Mrs Rooney's deceased sister's anniversary, isn't it?... you say –

REBEKAH. "That's a great idea".

SHERBORNE. [And then] –

REBEKAH. "Not having her badmouth me to anyone if she's doing that my god she will be sorry".

CAROLINE. "Have you got her number?" –

REBEKAH. "Yeah. Unless she's blocked me on that as well".

SHERBORNE. And then this...

CAROLINE. "If she does try to say that [you were responsible] or that it was me, and its undeniably obvious, what we'll do is say I left the company I was working for in Jan and one of the girls in the office has my old laptop that had your password saved on it so it will have been them and now you will have to change everything".

SHERBORNE. She's come up with a lie for you, hasn't she, if Mrs Rooney twigs that it's you? ... you say –

REBEKAH. "OK! I just don't know how she would ever know..."

SHERBORNE. ... And then... you pass on exactly what Caroline writes out as your script –

REBEKAH. "I've messaged her. I swear she better not cunt me off".

SHERBORNE. ... You're worried aren't you, because you really think that Mrs Rooney has worked out that you were responsible? Agreed?

REBEKAH. No.

(*The* **PUNDITS** *gather.*)

PUNDIT 1. Oooooh. Now that's actually exactly what Coleen was thinking.

PUNDIT 2. Yeah, and Coleen replies saying –

PUNDIT 1. No spoilers.

PUNDIT 2. Sorry, yeah. You've gotta hand it to Rebekah. Sherborne's onslaught is tough going but she's handling it. This court case lasted seven days, and Rebekah was on the stand for four of them.

PUNDIT 1. It was exhausting.

PUNDIT 2. It was. But Rebekah's come all this way. She's not gonna give up now. And finally, we're here. This is the moment where Wagatha Christie sets her trap. She reinstates Rebekah as a follower and begins uploading fake posts onto her private Instagram, seen only by –

PUNDIT 1. [...] /

PUNDIT 2. – / Rebek –

PUNDIT 1. [...] –

PUNDIT 2. / Rebekah Vardy's account.

(*The* **PUNDITS** *retreat.*)

SHERBORNE. ... 1251 ... [This is one of Coleen's] fake posts... the gender selection post... on Mrs Rooney's private instagram stories, [she] puts up –

COLEEN. "Lets go and see what this gender selection is all about".

SHERBORNE. Can you see? If you look down bottom left you'll see. Seen by one ...that's the @beckyvardy account?

REBEKAH. That's correct, yes.

SHERBORNE. [Then, published in *The Sun* some time later] ... 'Coleen Rooney is so desperate for her fifth baby to be a girl that she has looked into controversial gender selection treatment' ... Now we know, don't we, that [Mrs Rooney] going for gender selection... was fake?

REBEKAH. Yes.

SHERBORNE. But the paper doesn't know that... and neither does the source for it. True?

REBEKAH. Yes that's correct, although I don't recall seeing the image.

SHERBORNE. Let's look at this. Page 1854 ... 8 April, same day as the post, you message Ms Watt –

REBEKAH. "Coleen's Instagram wonder if they are going for baby 5".

SHERBORNE. And Caroline, who is ever on the case –

CAROLINE. "I already saw it. I can't believe she's posted it" –

REBEKAH. 'I know... maybe she's just put it to see if anyone gives it to the media' –

CAROLINE. 'I think that might be the case... attention seeking either way'.

SHERBORNE. Now, you see, [you have seen] the gender selection post.

REBEKAH. No. I recall a different image.

SHERBORNE. ... The reason you can't say that you saw this [is] because once you do, you are the only person who could have been responsible for that article, true or false?

REBEKAH. No, that's not true, my Lady...

SHERBORNE. ... Let's move on to the next [fake post] ... the flooded basement story. Page 752 ... Mrs Rooney wanted to put up one last fake post to confirm her suspicions. And so on 2nd October everyone bar your account was blocked, and she put this up... it's a bottle of wine, and it says –

COLEEN. 'Needed after today [...] flood in the basement of our new house [...] when it all seems to be going so well'.

SHERBORNE. ... *The Sun* [then] publish an article, don't they? ... 'Coleen Rooney has weathered plenty of storms during her eleven year marriage, but the latest one wasn't to do with husband Wayne. I can reveal last week's horrendous weather has wreaked havoc at the Rooney's £20 million family home, flooding their basement' ... Did you or did you not recall seeing [Mrs Rooney's post], Mrs Vardy?

REBEKAH. No, I don't recall seeing this.

SHERBORNE. You don't recall?

REBEKAH. No.

SHERBORNE. ... You said you don't remember seeing it. Can I take you to page 462? ... It is a response to Mrs Rooney's solicitors. They had asked a number of questions. Can you see?

REBEKAH. ... Yes.

SHERBORNE. ... And this is your answer... 'Mrs Vardy recalls seeing the flooded basement story'.

REBEKAH. ... A lot of things were – there was a lot of abuse during that time.

SHERBORNE. ... Mrs Vardy, I have to suggest to you that you are now trying to distance yourself from having seen that flooded basement post, aren't you?

REBEKAH. No.

SHERBORNE. And like the gender selection article and the car crash article, it was based on the information that you and Ms Watt passed through to *The Sun* and what you, and only you or Ms Watt, had seen on Mrs Rooney's private Instagram account. That's correct, isn't it?

REBEKAH. No, that's not correct.

STEYN. ... Would you like a break, Mrs Vardy?

REBEKAH. ... [Pause]

STEYN. Do you feel okay to continue?

REBEKAH. ... Yes.

SHERBORNE. ... The next thing that happens of course, is that Mrs Rooney puts up the post that is the subject of this action... that comes on 9th October... The 'reveal' post.

COLEEN. "For a few years now, someone who I trusted to follow me on my personal Instagram account" –

REBEKAH. Yes.

SHERBORNE. Can I take you to page 779 ... this is Caroline to you –

CAROLINE. ... "Message her now and ask what the fuck this is".

SHERBORNE. And then you say –

REBEKAH. ... "Wow. That's war".

SHERBORNE. And then she tells you what to say, doesn't she?

CAROLINE. "You will have to say that you don't speak to anyone about her but that recently your insta has even been following people you don't follow".

SHERBORNE. ... She's feeding you lines [again], isn't she, Mrs Vardy, to try and suggest to Mrs Rooney that you are not responsible, is that correct or not?

REBEKAH. No.

SHERBORNE. And then Caroline says –

CAROLINE. "I want to call her PR".

SHERBORNE. ... And then Caroline writes out what you should say to Coleen Rooney –

CAROLINE & REBEKAH. "As I have just said to you on the phone, I wish you had called me if you thought this. I never speak to anyone about you as various journalists who have asked me over the years can vouch for... I'm not being funny but I don't need the money, what would I gain from selling stories on you? I liked you a lot Coleen and I'm so upset that you have chosen to do this, especially when I'm heavily pregnant. I'm disgusted that I'm even having to deny this".

SHERBORNE. This is Caroline writing to you, what you should say?

REBEKAH. That's correct, because I couldn't think straight.

SHERBORNE. ... And [then] you put your story out... [an exclusive with *The Daily Mail*] '... Arguing with Coleen Rooney would be as pointless as arguing with a pigeon... You can tell it that you are right and it is wrong but it's still going to shit in your hair' ... That's what you said?

REBEKAH. I did, my Lady... this was initial, my initial response... in the midst of receiving some horrendous abuse. The last thing I was thinking of was... I was seven months pregnant.

SHERBORNE. I think we all understand that the abuse you got was awful. No one is saying anything differently. But... you chose to give an interview, an exclusive interview.

REBEKAH. That's correct, I had no joy in [talking to Coleen] on the phone, who refused to accept that and quite frankly revelled in my anguish.

(The **PUNDITS** *gather.)*

PUNDIT 2. Can you imagine it though? You look at your phone one afternoon and you see the entire internet is talking about *you.*

PUNDIT 1. Nobody's saying it wasn't stressful for her –

PUNDIT 2. Coleen obviously didn't care –

PUNDIT 1. This is about facts, not feelings.

PUNDIT 2. Yeah, well, the facts are that Rebekah's been questioned for *days* on this stand. She's had no respite.

PUNDIT 1. And it's not over yet. Because there's still one thing Sherborne still hasn't addressed. The evidence not before the court. Rebekah's missing messages.

(The **PUNDITS** *retreat.)*

SHERBORNE. ... Mrs Vardy, you are well aware... that we say there has been a catalogue of so-called unfortunate events which have befallen disclosure on your side?

REBEKAH. I've heard that a lot.

SHERBORNE. And you know that our case is that that's deliberate? [That] all of the WhatsApp images and audio files and video files, they've all been deleted?

REBEKAH. No, they weren't deleted. Something happened as I was exporting the whole file to my legal team.

SHERBORNE. We say 'delete', you say something odd happened. You see, Mrs Vardy, if you hadn't deleted all your messages –

REBEKAH. I didn't delete my messages. I disclosed my messages.

SHERBORNE. ... [You made sure] that we got no images or audio or video files from your messages with Ms Watt, didn't you?

REBEKAH. No, and that's extremely unfortunate because I still believe those messages and audio or whatever they would have been extremely helpful for this case.

SHERBORNE. ... So you say... [and] if Ms Watt's phone hadn't found its way to the bottom of the North sea, we'd be able to check it wouldn't we?

REBEKAH. Ms Watt disclosed.

SHERBORNE. No, Ms Watt has disclosed nothing that's relevant to this, has she, and you know that?

REBEKAH. I can't comment on that.

(**MR TOMLINSON** *stands.*)

TOMLINSON. Mr Sherborne is constantly commenting and making remarks to the witness. The witness has been in the box a long time. It is not very pleasant for him to be making comments.

STEYN. ... It is unnecessary and there's not really enough time for these comments in any event ... would you like a break, Mrs Vardy?

REBEKAH. ... No, I'm fine.

SHERBORNE. ... Mrs Vardy, we've seen in what disclosure we have managed to get from you and Ms Watt that you were consistently discussing, seeking to and indeed passing on information to *The Sun* about a number of people who were in your circle, information they wouldn't have wanted to make public, yes?

REBEKAH. No.

SHERBORNE. ... Would you not agree, Mrs Vardy, that if it looks like a leak and it sounds like a leak and you even use the world leak, that it is more likely than not to be a leak?

REBEKAH. No.

SHERBORNE. And that's what you were, a leak?

REBEKAH. No.

SHERBORNE. ... And that's why Ms Watt couldn't face coming to court in the end, to have been found that she lied, could she?

REBEKAH. Actually, I think she's been driven to suicidal thoughts by these proceedings and the antics of the defendant.

SHERBORNE. She even withdrew her statement being just read out. So we see in your second witness statement that you blame her instead and you say she may well have done it, after all these years of faithful service and doing only what you both knew and approved of her doing; isn't that correct?

REBEKAH. No.

SHERBORNE. You see, Mrs Vardy, I have to put it to you that it is not her that betrayed you, as you suggest. It is you that has betrayed her by throwing her under the bus.

REBEKAH. Is that a joke?

SHERBORNE. Let's see what the court says, Mrs Vardy. I have no further questions.

(**SHERBORNE** *sits.* **TOMLINSON** *stands.*)

STEYN. Thank you. Mr Tomlinson?

TOMLINSON. Thank you... Mrs Vardy... it is obviously very difficult, and nobody expects you to remember the fine detail of things that happened years ago, Mrs Vardy, but... how often did you discuss Mrs Rooney's private Instagram account with Ms Watt?

REBEKAH. It was a handful of times.

TOMLINSON. ... Now, I do not want to spend a lot of time on this but... the *News of the World* article about Mr Peter Andre –

REBEKAH. There's a lot things in [the article] that didn't come out my mouth, that were misrepresented and the circumstances around that article, which I'm deeply sorry for and I've apologised for this. And it's shameful reading that, it's one of my biggest regrets.

TOMLINSON. ... Now, I want to come to the topic of deletion... have you, at any stage, deliberately deleted anything from your WhatsApp messages, Mrs Vardy?

REBEKAH. No, never.

TOMLINSON. ... What was your state of mind when you [exported the WhatsApp messages]?

REBEKAH. I wasn't very well. I was having constant panic attacks, anxiety, and I was scared I was going to lose my baby.

TOMLINSON. ... Finally, Mrs Vardy... did you personally... leak information from any of those posts to *The Sun*?

REBEKAH. No I didn't, my Lady.

TOMLINSON. Have you ever asked Ms Caroline Watt whether she has leaked any of this information?

REBEKAH. Yes, I did... pretty much all the way through these proceedings.

TOMLINSON. And what did she say?

REBEKAH. She said no.

TOMLINSON. ... How have you found... the process of cross-examination and giving evidence in this court?

REBEKAH. Exhausting. Intimidating. I feel like I've been bullied and manipulated.

TOMLINSON. ... But you chose to go on... why was that, Mrs Vardy?

REBEKAH. Because I didn't do anything wrong and I wanted to clear my name, and not just for me, but for my family and for my children.

TOMLINSON. Thank you, Mrs Vardy. I have no more questions.

> (**MR TOMLINSON** *sits.*)

> (*The* **PUNDITS** *gather.*)

PUNDIT 1. After nearly four days on the stand, that's the end of Rebekah Vardy's evidence. Impressive stamina for a fatigued player, but I think we can all agree – this game is sewn up. To use Rebekah's own words – ha ha, she defo did it.

PUNDIT 2. Jeff, we don't *know* that –

PUNDIT 1. Come on, the WhatsApps. The leaks. Caroline literally saying 'It was me'!

PUNDIT 2. But that's not why we're in court. We're not here to see if Rebekah sold stories on Riyad Mahrez or anyone else. We are here to determine if what Coleen posted on social media was true or not. We are here for *the evidence.*

PUNDIT 1. But if she's willing to sell stories on Riyad Mahrez, Danny Drinkwater, and national treasure Peter Andre – then why not Coleen?

PUNDIT 2. That's not evidence. And remember, it's hard to win a libel case in the UK if you're the publisher. It's hard to win if you're Coleen Rooney.

PUNDIT 1. So Wagatha Christie needs to come back fighting after half-time.

PUNDIT 2. Because if she doesn't –

PUNDIT 1. Then Rebekah Vardy's won.

(**STEYN** *blows the whistle.*)

(*Half time.*)

2.

(... Lights up on the same scene.)

*(The **PUNDITS** gather.)*

PUNDIT 1. And welcome back. I've just about caught my breath after a gripping first half, what about you, Jem?

PUNDIT 2. Vardy's not covered herself in glory, I'll admit, but the game isn't over yet. And while Rebekah had to defend Coleen's legal attack, the tables are about to turn.

PUNDIT 1. I'm not worried, Coleen's a cerebral player.

PUNDIT 2. She is, but she's been on the bench for all of Vardy's marathon performance. Coleen might not be match fit, Jeff.

PUNDIT 1. I reckon she is. We've had reports that she's been writing the odd thing down in a notebook. She's prepped, she's ready for this.

PUNDIT 2. She can make all the notes she wants, the question still remains – can she prove that what she said in her post was true?

*(**PUNDITS** touch earpieces.)*

PUNDIT 1. Luckily for her, she doesn't have to do it alone. Because every great detective needs a sidekick. Mulder had Scully. Holmes had Watson.

PUNDIT 2. And – yep – Coleen's got a secret weapon of her own.

(**STEYN** *blows the whistles. The second half commences.*)

SHERBORNE. With your Ladyship's permission, I call our next witness, Wayne Rooney.

(**PUNDIT 1** *becomes* **WAYNE ROONEY**.)

(**WAYNE ROONEY** *raises his hand.*)

Mr Rooney, can you give your full name to the court, please.

WAYNE. Wayne Rooney.

SHERBORNE. And I am going to say this, but I think so far you're doing well, if I may say, if you can keep your voice up as much as possible and also if you can direct your answers to her Ladyship. Thank you... on page 334 ...a document entitled 'Witness statement of Wayne Rooney' ...do you see a signature?

WAYNE. I do.

SHERBORNE. Is it your signature?

WAYNE. Yes, it is.

SHERBORNE. Thank you Mr Rooney. Can you just confirm then, to the best of your knowledge and belief, is that witness statement true?

WAYNE. It is.

SHERBORNE. If you just stay there, Mr Rooney, Mr Tomlinson will have some questions.

(**SHERBORNE** *sits.* **TOMLINSON** *stands.*)

TOMLINSON. Good morning, Mr Rooney.

WAYNE. Good morning.

TOMLINSON. ... First of all, I'd like to ask you about Instagram. Am I right in thinking you have a private Instagram account? ... Is that 'wazzaroon08'?

WAYNE. Yes, that is correct.

TOMLINSON. ... And you're a follower of your wife's private Instagram account?

WAYNE. That is correct.

TOMLINSON. ... You say in your witness statement that you recall that your wife was frustrated by posts and stories on her private Instagram being leaked to *The Sun*?

WAYNE. That is correct.

TOMLINSON. And you go on to say that you didn't want to get involved?

WAYNE. That is correct.

TOMLINSON. What do you mean by that, Mr Rooney?

WAYNE. ... I'm not big on social media and I didn't want to get involved. I think my wife is an independent woman who does her own thing.

TOMLINSON. I mean, obviously you want to make sure your wife is happy and to protect her against things that she finds difficult or unpleasant?

WAYNE. Yes, that is correct.

TOMLINSON. So if she's saying to you there's something which is disturbing her... don't you want to help her?

WAYNE. Yeah, and I believe I helped my wife. We have four children we look after. Social media, for me, is the least of them worries.

TOMLINSON. ... Wasn't it a matter of some concern to you if *The Sun* was getting hold of private information relating to your family?

WAYNE. ... It's always a matter of concern when it involves your family. I think there was information which my wife said had been leaked. There was information which was fake, which was out there in the public, and that is something we – myself, my wife have had to deal with since we were sixteen years of age... as I explain, my wife was dealing with it in her own way which I was completely unaware of.

TOMLINSON. ... So through the time your wife was doing this she never mentioned anything to you, is that your evidence?

WAYNE. That is correct, my wife didn't mention any posts, anything she was doing. I was completely – I had no knowledge of that... [The reveal post was] my first time seeing it... I woke up – I'm not sure of the date but the date of the reveal post... I was in the US, my wife was in England and I seen it I think... about two p.m... I seen my wife had put a post out and that was the first knowledge I had of that... me sitting in this courtroom... is the first time I'm hearing almost everything on this case...

(*The* **PUNDITS** *gather.*)

PUNDIT 2. Not exactly the detective partnership Coleen had hoped for.

PUNDIT 1. Turns out Wagatha works alone. Still, every good mystery needs a red herring.

PUNDIT 2. But Tomlinson's not giving up just yet. He's about to take Wayne back to that fateful Euros 2016, to try and prove his theory that the Rooneys had a vendetta against Rebekah Vardy. But Wayne Rooney's not for turning.

(*The* **PUNDITS** *retreat.*)

TOMLINSON. ... [Something else] you deal with in your witness statement... what happened at the Euros

2016. And I think it is right that you were the England captain during that tournament?

WAYNE. I was.

TOMLINSON. And that Mr Jamie Vardy was also one of the England squad?

WAYNE. He was.

TOMLINSON. And as with all English tournaments, there was a lot of media attention to what was going on with the players and also their wives, girlfriend and partners and so on?

WAYNE. There was.

TOMLINSON. ... And at one stage, you say you were pulled aside by a member of FA staff and asked to speak to Mr Vardy?

WAYNE. That is correct... that was the England manager, Roy Hodgson and his assistant manager, Gary Neville.

TOMLINSON. ... And what did they say to you, Mr Rooney?

WAYNE. So they asked me to – as a captain – would I be able to speak to Mr Vardy on issues regarding his wife... So I agreed to speak to Mr Vardy and ask... his wife to calm down and not bring any issues off the field.

TOMLINSON. 'Ask his wife to calm down', I mean she wasn't dancing on tables... What kind of calming down are we talking about, Mr Rooney?

WAYNE. No, she wasn't as far as I am aware. But it was... [there was] a lot of media coverage, and obviously as the manager of England, [Roy Hodgson] didn't want that to happen and he asked me if I would be able to speak to Jamie, which I went and done.

TOMLINSON. ... page 332, At paragraph 3, you say –

WAYNE. 'I think Becky had some kind of column in *The Sun* about Euro 2016'.

TOMLINSON. ... Was it forbidden to have a column in *The Sun*?

WAYNE. No, it wasn't.

TOMLINSON. ... So she had a perfectly permissible column in *The Sun*, and that was what you were complaining about?

WAYNE. I didn't complain about it. I was asked to carry out an instruction. [Rebekah] had the column in *The Sun*. There was – amongst the players before the tournament, and this isn't set in law but it was spoken that no one have any distractions. We didn't want any newspaper columns, any articles, and that's a conversation we had as a group of players.

TOMLINSON. ... Are you saying that her column in *The Sun* was a distraction? Is that your evidence?

WAYNE. No, I was asked to speak to Mr Vardy by the England manager and assistant manager, and I carried out that instruction. I was aware it was an awkward situation for me. I'm sure it was an awkward situation for Mr Vardy but... I carried out that instruction.

TOMLINSON. ... You've seen documents referred to where Mrs Vardy asked her husband whether it was true that you'd spoken to him?

WAYNE. Yes.

TOMLINSON. And he'd said no?

WAYNE. I'm aware of that.

TOMLINSON. And do you remember a time when you were with [Jamie] and he was... Facetiming [Mrs Vardy], who was asking him, is it right Wayne's been told to tell you off? And he said no, and he got you on the screen and you said the same thing to her. Do you remember?

WAYNE. I don't recall... that conversation taking place. What I do recall is Mrs Vardy was on FaceTime a lot throughout the tournament with Jamie, the lads – we had down time, we played darts, we played pool etc. Mrs Vardy was almost there with the team... I know I spoke to Jamie Vardy 100%. Whether Jamie goes on to give that information to his wife, that's entirely his business... if he didn't tell his wife, that's down to him.

TOMLINSON. ... You see, Mr Rooney, I think I am suggesting you're wrong about that, that you didn't actually raise it with Mr Vardy because there was actually nothing to raise?

WAYNE. I'm sat here under oath, I 100% spoke to Mr Vardy... I remember Mr Vardy had a can of Red Bull, I had a coffee. I remember... because it was such an awkward moment for me to have to speak to him.

TOMLINSON. ... Thank you, Mr Rooney.

*(**MR TOMLINSON** sits. **SHERBORNE** stands.)*

SHERBORNE. Mr Rooney... you have been in court here throughout these proceedings supporting your wife. Can I ask you this – did she want to be sitting in this court?

WAYNE. I don't think anyone wants to be in this court. I certainly don't and I know me wife doesn't want to be in court in this situation. I've watched me wife over the last two, two and a half years, really struggle with everything what's gone on, become a different mother, a different wife. It's been very traumatic for my wife through this situation and hopefully whatever the judgement is on this case myself, me wife and our children can go on and live our lives because its not something we've wanted to be part of.

SHERBORNE. Thank you, Mr Rooney. I have no further questions.

(As **WAYNE ROONEY** *stands –.)*

STEYN. ... I just have one question. [You're] a follower of your wife's private Instagram account?

WAYNE. Yes.

STEYN. There was a stage when a number of – she was putting up a number of posts that were false and presumably you would have known they were false. Did you see any of those?

SHERBORNE. Could I – sorry, Mr Rooney could be released but I just... the fake posts were hidden from everyone bar –

STEYN. Yes. Ah yes, you're absolutely right. Thank you. Yes, please do sit down.

(The **PUNDITS** *gather.)*

PUNDIT 2. Yeah, that actually happened.

PUNDIT 1. OK, back to the main event. Because, let's face it, there's only one Rooney we really want to hear from. She's the reason we're all here today. It's time to hear from Wagatha Christie herself.

(The **PUNDITS** *retreat.)*

SHERBORNE. With your Ladyship's permission, [can I call] Mrs Rooney.

*(***COLEEN ROONEY** *takes the stand.)*

STEYN. Thank you, do take a seat.

COLEEN. Thank you.

SHERBORNE. ... Mrs Rooney, can you give your full name to the court, please?

COLEEN. Coleen Rooney.

SHERBORNE. I say this to every witness, so please don't take this personally... try and remember to keep your voice as loud as possible... I think it is page 278 ... You should find a document there entitled 'Witness Statement of Coleen Rooney'.

COLEEN. Yes.

SHERBORNE. ... And you can confirm that, to the best of your knowledge and belief, that this evidence is true?

COLEEN. Yes.

> (**MR SHERBORNE** *sits*. **MR TOMLINSON** *stands*.)

TOMLINSON. Mrs Rooney... D1 ...page 1215 ... That's the post that you put up on 9th October 2019. [The reveal post].

COLEEN. It is.

TOMLINSON. What were you trying to achieve by putting that post up, Mrs Rooney?

COLEEN. I wasn't trying to – I wasn't achieving anything. What I wanted was to stop the person who was leaking my private information to *The Sun*. I'd give out warning signs many a times, it didn't stop. This was my last resort.

TOMLINSON. ... Obviously you knew it was going to cause a massive impact across millions of people, correct?

COLEEN. No, I was surprised myself how much interest it caused.

TOMLINSON. Well, you have millions of followers on social media, don't you? And you posted this on Twitter, Instagram and Facebook... to make sure it reached as many people as possible?

COLEEN. Yes.

TOMLINSON. And you knew, didn't you, that it would be picked up by media?

COLEEN. To be honest with you – well, sorry for using that, but yes, I do. My life has been picked up by the media for the last twenty years, no matter how big or small the things I do, so obviously it was going to get picked up by the media.

TOMLINSON. But it wasn't about you. It was about Rebekah Vardy.

COLEEN. Rebekah Vardy was involved in this and it was about me as well.

TOMLINSON. ... [So we can] agree that in [the reveal post], you are accusing Rebekah Vardy of being the person responsible for leaking private information to *The Sun*?

COLEEN. I – yes. I mention Rebekah's name. I mention Rebekah's account.

TOMLINSON. ... [But] it was understood, wasn't it, that you were making an accusation against Rebekah Vardy personally?

COLEEN. ... Yes, that's what the newspapers reported.

TOMLINSON. ... You say in the [reveal] post, "There has been so much information given to [*The Sun*] about me and my friends and my family – all without my permission or knowledge". ... The car crash [article]... A dent in the side of a car... is that private information about yourself, friends and family?

COLEEN. Yes, the story that was written, I remember, I was in America at the time, which was a terrible time for me. I've never moved more than forty five minutes up the road. I'm a family person. My friends and family mean the world to me. My mum and dad have literally brought up my children with me. The fact that I went and lived in America was – I've never believed in home sickness before until I got there. I cried every single night... so on that photograph, I... went online and there was a story in *The Sun*, and straightaway I knew it came from... my private Instagram. There was no crash.... a lorry literally scraped down the side of my car. No kids were in the car, no family.... and I was annoyed, I was, you know, I was fuming.

TOMLINSON. ... [And] in the context of press enquiries... [your representative] said it's 'a minor bump six weeks ago' ... so for six weeks you've been driving – and this is not a criticism, Mrs Rooney – you've been driving round in a car with a bump down one side?

COLEEN. Yes.

TOMLINSON. And the car has been on the street, in the road, in the garage, you've been taking the kids to school?

COLEEN. Yes?

TOMLINSON. ... So anybody could have seen the scrape down the side? ... You don't know... whether the source of the story is the [Instagram] post –

COLEEN. ... 'RIP Half a Honda' –

TOMLINSON. ... or whether the source of the story is some completely different person? *The Sun* could have been told, 'Coleen Rooney has got a bash on her car'?

COLEEN. They could have, yes.

TOMLINSON. ... What other information are we talking about, Mrs Rooney?

COLEEN. ... So the pyjamas post... so on my public Instagram, we have – we're patrons of Alder Hey Hospital in Liverpool. Every year, they do a pyjama campaign with Matalan, so we take a photograph and put it on social media to support the campaign. And on my public Instagram, I put up a photograph of me and the children in the pyjamas... at that time, my relationship with my husband – there had been a situation which was, you know, it was wrongdoing by my husband. I was in a vulnerable situation. I didn't know how my marriage was going to work out... on my private Instagram, I put a picture of my husband with the children... and the headline in *The Sun* was 'Guess who's back in the big bed' or 'He's back in the big bed' ... But I didn't want the public to know that. I hadn't settled on a – you know, this is it, we're getting back together... so I kept it within my close circle, but obviously, the post got given to *The Sun*.

TOMLINSON.   Yes, okay... the fact that you and your husband were on speaking terms, or on better terms than some people in the public think, is [another] piece of private information... apart from [that and the car crash article] Mrs Rooney, [what are] the other [leaked posts] about your family and friends?

> (*The* **PUNDITS** *gather.*)

PUNDIT 2.   We can definitely skip this. This is just Coleen listing real posts that she believed ended up in *The Sun*. All small fry, low level snippets of information about her life. And like Tomlinson says, Coleen has no proof that these stories necessarily came from her private Instagram in the first place, so –

PUNDIT 1.   Not so fast. This is all part of Coleen's investigation. It was these leaked posts that led her to believe she had a follower selling information to the press. This is the genesis of her plan.

PUNDIT 2. Not really relevant to –

PUNDIT 1. I think it's important, Jem –

PUNDIT 2. *This* action, which is about –

> (**PUNDIT 1** *touches their earpiece.*)

PUNDIT 1. And yep, I can confirm these were... the post about Wayne's birthday, the post about trick or treating at Halloween, the post about the Rooney's finally getting a babysitter when they lived in America.

PUNDIT 2. Again, not actually relevant to this court case, which is about the –

PUNDIT 1. Wait, yeah, to give you a flavour – here's Coleen talking about some posts she put up at a well-known private members club –

(Live action replay – we're on **COLEEN.***)*

COLEEN. ... Take the Soho Farmhouse... you're not meant to take photographs and put it in public, you know, while you're there... that's why I put [pictures] on my private Instagram... It's the way they got made out to look... my friend was drinking beer in front of children and families... I was driving at high speed on a bicycle with a bottle of wine, but then [*The Sun*] give a dig at my husband, who had been done for drink driving –

(Live action replay ends.)

PUNDIT 2. We all know that Coleen believed there was a leak on her Instagram account, which led her to conduct her own investigation. But she had *zero evidence* this was Rebekah Vardy... so why was it *only her* who Coleen targeted?

(The **PUNDITS** *retreat.)*

TOMLINSON. The same day as the [car crash] article... You published... a cry of rage or complaint on your Instagram...

COLEEN. "Someone on here is selling stories again to this scum of a paper".

TOMLINSON. Then... you decide to review the accounts of your followers on your private Instagram account... That's quite a job, isn't it, Mrs Rooney?

COLEEN. It was.

TOMLINSON. Because you've got three hundred accounts to review, something like that? ...did you make a record of this exercise? Did you write anything down? Was it all in your head?

COLEEN. No. It's quite easy to do on a phone.

TOMLINSON. And you unfollow [Mrs Vardy] in early February? ...You decide that she's had a lot of exclusives with *The Sun*.

COLEEN. ... A number of them, yes. It's quite easy to just go on Google. I Googled 'Exclusives. Rebekah Vardy. *Sun* Newspaper' and a lot come up.

TOMLINSON. ... Your complaints, Mrs Rooney, appear to be directed at the way that *The Sun* treats the stories rather than the nature of the information. ... *The Sun* Newspaper, Mrs Rooney, has treated you very badly over the years, hasn't it?

COLEEN. ... Yes, we've had our share of not nice stories.

TOMLINSON. And 2019 was a particularly bad year, wasn't it? ... There's day after day, sometimes two or three a day, of articles about you and your husband, with people who are claiming to have inside knowledge talking about what you think and what he thinks and what's going on in your life?

COLEEN. ... They have done it for years. 2019 doesn't stand out as any different to any other year.

TOMLINSON. ... Isn't your real complaint about... the way that *The Sun* has treated you?

COLEEN. No... This case is that someone was leaking my private information to *The Sun* newspaper. ... The matter is that my private information that I put up on my Instagram was getting given to someone else.

TOMLINSON. ... Some of [your 300 followers] are obviously your old friends. Some of them, forgive me for using this term, it's slightly derogatory sometimes... some of them are WAGS?

COLEEN. Wives and girlfriends of fellow football players –

TOMLINSON. ... And some of [these WAGS] will have PRs, I mean, not just Rebekah Vardy some of them will have agents or PRs who will have access to their Instagram accounts. You have had, for many years, a relationship with Mr Stretford's [PR] company and also with [Rachel Monk at] Monk PR. Is that right?

COLEEN. Yes that's correct... what happened, at the beginning was, obviously my husband was playing football professionally. I was papped going to school when I was sixteen years old. There was interest from that photograph and a lot of work offers came in. I was at school at the time... so obviously, the first person they would go to was Wayne's agent [Paul Stretford] ... So since that day onwards, he has just always managed stuff for me that has come in... but we – me and Rebekah have totally different ways of working. Obviously, Rebekah was friendly with Caroline Watt, that's totally different to my relationship with people who I work with.

TOMLINSON. ... Paragraph sixteen of your witness statement –

COLEEN. "... Broadly speaking I only accept [follow] requests from people who are close to me, and people I trust... even if one of the followers of the private Instagram account is a business account... it will likely be because I have a connection to the owner of that business".

TOMLINSON. ... Obviously people who have business Instagram accounts will have employees, or some of them will have employees who will operate their accounts?

COLEEN. Most of the time, yes, but these are independent businesses Puro Juice is one girl who makes juice, Kelly, from her home... "kathryndesignerkids" ... I've known Kathryn for years, she's the owner of a kids clothes shop... it's one person involved in that. Rise Fitness is my brother's account. All the businesses have got a connection to me...

TOMLINSON. Some of them, as I've said before, are WAGS –

COLEEN. Wives and girlfriends of fellow football players –

TOMLINSON. Yes, it's a very disrespectful term.

COLEEN. No, it's not very disrespectful, it's just a word that I don't use.

TOMLINSON. ... As I've said... some of these people will have PRs... who have access to their Instagram accounts? ... In relation to your public account, I think your brother controls that, doesn't he?

COLEEN. Yes.

TOMLINSON. ... So my point is a simple one, Mrs Rooney... you can't be sure that someone else is not responsible? [But] in this case your suspicions have focused on Mrs Vardy?

COLEEN. ... In this case, I believe that account was the one that was responsible... I've been in the public eye for twenty years. I've been around this. I've become quite savvy to the way people work and journalists work.

TOMLINSON. ... But if someone else had access to her account... The right thing to do was... to warn her that this was going on? ... why didn't you pick up the phone? ... Why didn't you get in touch with her at that stage?

COLEEN. I've never picked up the phone to Rebekah Vardy... the only time I've spoken to her is on the day of the post. That's the only time I've spoken to her on the phone.

TOMLINSON. Yes –

COLEEN. But on that blocking – ... I thought, do you know what, just block.

TOMLINSON. ... Mrs Vardy's message to you [after being unfollowed] –

REBEKAH. "Hi my love... hope you are all OK? I saw you had unfollowed me and I wasn't following you anymore on Instagram... just wanted to ask if I had done something or offended you in anyway? Literally only just noticed the other day".

TOMLINSON. And you replied by telling a lie, didn't you? ... You reply –

COLEEN. ... "Oh I didn't even know. The kids have my phone all the time and have probably done it. Let me check".

TOMLINSON. ... Why weren't you honest, Mrs Rooney?

COLEEN. ... Because I didn't want to be. Because I had put warning signs out there... I know it sounds a bit tough but at that time I didn't think she would tell the truth anyway, even if I confronted her.

TOMLINSON. ... You wanted to trap her?

COLEEN. ... No, not a trap. I just wanted to find out who was doing this to me. I thought by going public on Twitter and saying someone is doing this to me... that would be, you know, the end of it... they continued, they carried on. So I felt the only way... is to continue trying to catch the person out myself.

TOMLINSON. ... You have no idea as to whether Mrs Vardy was responsible for the leaking of these posts, do you? She may have been, she may not have been.

COLEEN. I don't know... having looked at the material I've had since –

TOMLINSON. ... We're not talking about what you knew since. We're talking about the [reveal] post.

COLEEN. Yes, with that post, a lot of stuff that I gathered beforehand, just it all added up, that the messages that Mrs Vardy sent me were always direct. I never sent her messages, and that was not being unfriendly, that was just that she was not in my, you know, circle of friends. I felt like when she contacted me, it was always to try and get information out of me. A lot of the time it was when there was something not nice going on with my personal life, and she used to say "are you okay?" Which at the beginning I thought was genuinely nice, but towards the end, I felt like it was a bit unusual.

TOMLINSON. ... Yes.... You have a section in your witness statement headed –

COLEEN. "Becky's relationship with me" –

TOMLINSON. ... You say, with hindsight, she was trying too hard?

COLEEN. Not at the beginning, no. Our first contact I think... was I got invited to her wedding. Obviously Wayne and Jamie had played together... we couldn't make it, it was a busy time of year... and I sent a gift and that's – I think Rebekah then replied to say thank you for that.

TOMLINSON. ... ... If you look at page 1888... It is a series of WhatsApp messages between you and Mrs Vardy... [after] another apparent crisis in your relationship with your husband... there were newspaper reports about your husband misbehaving?

COLEEN. ... We've dealt with it as a couple, as a family and yes there was a few things that had been published over them few years.

TOMLINSON. ... There's a message on the 27th August from Mrs Vardy to you –

REBEKAH. "Hope you're okay, you're a tough girl, keep smiling, sending hugs".

TOMLINSON. ... There's nothing suspicious about that message, is there, Mrs Rooney?

COLEEN. ... I felt like it was a bit of fishing for information.

TOMLINSON. ... And you responded later that morning –

COLEEN. "Congratulations on your brilliant news. Hope it all goes well for you".

TOMLINSON. Because she was pregnant?

COLEEN. Yes.

TOMLINSON. So in quite a potentially vulnerable state?

COLEEN. I wouldn't have thought she was vulnerable. Pregnancy, you know it's – I didn't think there was anything wrong with her. I hadn't seen reports of her being vulnerable... I was being genuine, as a woman even though I had suspicions I would never ever wish, you know, any harm while anyone was pregnant, and that was genuine congratulations.

TOMLINSON. ... Let's go to the next heading in your witness statement –

COLEEN. '[Becky's] Desire to be Famous'

TOMLINSON. ... How is that evidence that she is leaking from your private Instagram account?

COLEEN. ... My view is that she wants to be kept relevant.

TOMLINSON. ... [Because] *The Sun* decided [to have] Mrs Vardy do columns on what was going on at the [Euro] tournament? ... You used to write I think a column, was it for *Closer* magazine?

COLEEN. Yes.

TOMLINSON. ... There's nothing questionable about that, is there?

COLEEN. I've got nothing wrong with whatever Mrs Vardy wanted to do. It's fine as long as it's nothing to do with me.

TOMLINSON. ... So you've got three pieces of evidence. You've got one, some exclusives in *The Sun*, you've got two, desire to be famous... which is largely about staged pap shots... and you've got three, the fact that she sends you messages you think are a bit odd? That's the only evidence you rely on.

COLEEN. Yes.

TOMLINSON. ... You see, the truth is this, Mrs Rooney, isn't it, you do not actually have any evidence to link Mrs Vardy to the leaking of material from your private Instagram, do you?

COLEEN. ... I believe that Mrs Vardy knew that this was happening.

TOMLINSON. What you believe, Mrs Rooney, isn't evidence. I might believe that Derby County will win the Premiership in two years time, but it's not evidence that they're going to.

COLEEN. No, it's not.

TOMLINSON. ... You said in the [reveal] post... "I saved and screenshotted the original stories" ...But we don't actually have any screenshots... from April 2019, do we?

COLEEN. No, not in my camera roll.

TOMLINSON. You have deleted them.

COLEEN. ... I'm not sure because –

TOMLINSON. ... Page 1286 ... [That's your third Instagram story] on 24th August... do you know what's happened to the other two? They haven't been produced.

COLEEN. I can't recall.

TOMLINSON. Have they been deleted?

COLEEN. Not that I know of. I don't know.

TOMLINSON. ... Go to the previous page... it's your reaction to the gender selection article... it's the first of two [Instagram stories that day]. Do you know where the other one is?

COLEEN. No.

TOMLINSON. ... You'll understand, Mrs Rooney, why I'm making these points, because in your case it's been constantly said that the fact there's a missing document indicates that Mrs Vardy has deliberately concealed wrongdoing.

COLEEN. Yes.

TOMLINSON. And yet... there are documents... from your Instagram [and phone] which have gone missing. I'm not suggesting you've deliberately concealed them, but sometimes things go missing when you're operating with electronic documents, don't they?

COLEEN. Sometimes.

TOMLINSON. ... Sometimes, things get deleted for perfectly innocent reasons. You agree?

COLEEN. Yes, sometimes they do.

TOMLINSON. [Yet] I'm not suggesting you [deleted documents] deliberately.

COLEEN. ... Yes, I ... [But] things went missing not just from Mrs Vardy but Caroline Watt... I do understand sometimes mishaps happen, but not that much.

TOMLINSON. Like the whole of your WhatsApp, because you changed phones and that went missing?

COLEEN. Yes.

TOMLINSON. ... You say, [in the reveal post] going down the page on 1216 –

COLEEN. ... "Over the past five months, I have posted a series of false stories to see if they made their way into *The Sun* newspaper. And you know what? They did..."

TOMLINSON. ... That gives the impression that [all] your false stories all ended up in *The Sun*? ... That's not true, is it? ...

COLEEN. No... Not all of them.

TOMLINSON. ... Page 1280 ... This is a [false] post about setting up an events company. That never made it into *The Sun*, did it?

COLEEN. No.

TOMLINSON. ... If you go the next page, there's –

COLEEN. "Going to be a housewarming!"

TOMLINSON. Was that true?

COLEEN. No.

TOMLINSON. ... So that's a [false] post that went nowhere... a few pages on –

COLEEN. "Wedding vibes. Planning".

TOMLINSON. ... And –

COLEEN. ... "Escaping the measles outbreak in Washington".

TOMLINSON. Did [those false posts] make it into *The Sun*?

COLEEN. No.

TOMLINSON. ... No... I think disclosure has been given seventeen stories. Are you aware of that? ... [But] the data download appears to show that there was in fact fifty stories that you posted... only to Rebekah Vardy's account.

COLEEN. It was definitely not fifty ... I'm not sure how many there was all in all –

TOMLINSON. ... And only one ended up in *The Sun*?

*(The **PUNDITS** gather.)*

PUNDIT 2. He shoots. He scores.

PUNDIT 1. Nah, that's not right.

PUNDIT 2. That is a goal. The data shows that Coleen uploaded fifty false stories – sometimes posting several times a day – in order to catch Rebekah Vardy. She was obsessed with it being Rebekah –

PUNDIT 1. It probably wasn't quite fifty stories. And more than one ended up in *The Sun*.

PUNDIT 2. Let's take a look at that again –

(Live action replay.)

TOMLINSON. ... And only one ended up in *The Sun*?

COLEEN. No, at the time I believe three ended up on *The Sun*, but now obviously with the TV decisions, with one getting took out, I believe two ended up in *The Sun*... TV decisions isn't in my [case] ...no more.

*(The **PUNDITS** gather, fingers on earpieces.)*

PUNDIT 2. You heard it right there. Of all those fake stories, only two actually ended up in *The Sun*. But if we remember from the reveal post, Coleen accused Rebekah of leaking three –

*(Live action replay – we're on **COLEEN**.)*

COLEEN. "... And you know what, they did! The story about gender selection in Mexico, the story about returning to TV and then the latest story about the basement flooding in my new house".

PUNDIT 1. Now the post in question about returning to TV – called the 'TV decisions' post – was published to Coleen's private Instagram stories, to only Rebekah Vardy's account –

COLEEN. "Up and out!!! Easing my way back into work. TV decisions today. Maybe it's time for Australia?"

PUNDIT 1. OK and – sometime later – the story about 'TV decisions' made its way into the papers. It was only seen by one account – Rebekah Vardy's – so it's fair enough for Coleen to assume that Rebekah leaked it.

PUNDIT 2. Assumptions aren't facts. If you remember, Rebekah and Caroline waived their right to source protection and in relation to the gender selection and flooded basement posts – no journalists came forward. But on the TV decisions post, one journalist did. Mr Hamilton. He said that neither of the women were the source. He said Caroline and Rebekah were innocent.

PUNDIT 1. OK, fine. But like Coleen just said, it's not in her case anymore. And she's still got the other two fake posts. The basement flooding, the gender selection –

PUNDIT 2. But if Coleen got it wrong about the TV decisions post, how can we believe any of her accusations are true?

*(The **PUNDITS** retreat.)*

TOMLINSON. ... Paragraph 106 you say this –

COLEEN. "For the avoidance of any doubt, I did not mention the plan or the content of the Sting Operation to anyone or discuss it in person at any time".

TOMLINSON. ... Why didn't you discuss it with anybody?

COLEEN. Because I – one thing I don't do is put my troubles or my worries on anyone else. I've done that always.

TOMLINSON. ... The gender selection article... [Rachel Monk from Monk PR, contacts you to say] "they're running a story tomorrow about you going for gender selection in Mexico" ... And you say –

COLEEN. "Rachel give me a call".

TOMLINSON. What did you tell her to say to *The Sun*?

COLEEN. I said say you can't get hold of me or just say nothing at all...

TOMLINSON. You *wanted* the story to run?

COLEEN. ... Well... she said they were going to run it because they had a screenshot anyway.

TOMLINSON. ... This was really a serious and concerted operation, wasn't it, Mrs Rooney?

COLEEN. No... it's been made out a lot bigger than what it actually is.

TOMLINSON. ... So then... you have the idea of putting up a fake post saying your basement has been flooded.

COLEEN. ... Yes.

TOMLINSON. ... And then the flooded basement article was published [in *The Sun*] ... And it was at that stage you decided to put up the [reveal] post, is that right?

COLEEN. ... Oh, it was the next day, yes.

TOMLINSON. ... I mean you were obviously monitoring *The Sun*, because you saw it as soon as it came up on the – even before it was in the paper in the morning, you were checking online?

COLEEN. Yes... I do Google news and I put my name in and click news.

TOMLINSON. ... You said in your witness statement that you started writing this in... pen and paper?

COLEEN. Yes... I always have a notebook, I jot down a lot of things. I'm known to have a notebook and a piece of paper and a diary.

TOMLINSON. ... But you wrote it like a whodunnit, you know, with the... It's [..........] Rebekah Vardy's account. It was done to grab attention, wasn't it?

COLEEN. I use dots a lot... so it was just the way I wrote it, it come natural to me.

TOMLINSON. ... And very shortly afterward [you publish the reveal post], [Mrs Vardy] messaged you on WhatsApp, didn't she? ... and she says –

REBEKAH. "WTF is this?"

TOMLINSON. And you say –

COLEEN. "You know what this is".

TOMLINSON. And she says she's got no idea... and she makes it clear to you that it wasn't her, doesn't she?

COLEEN. Yes she says she has no interest in what's going on in my life, which I believe is totally untrue.

TOMLINSON. [Then] ... This is a post by you... on your private Instagram.

COLEEN. ... "Don't play games with a girl who can play better".

TOMLINSON. ... You were absolutely determined you were going to out her, weren't you? ... On the 9th October, you were going to reveal to the world that Rebekah Vardy was the villain?

COLEEN. No not the villain. She was the person who was passing... personal information to the press. Whether it be Rebekah Vardy or Kelly who makes the juices, I would out them anyway.

TOMLINSON. ... And meanwhile you had a massive reaction on social media, yes?

COLEEN. Yes, there was.

TOMLINSON. ... People were posting all kinds of photos and memes...talking about 'Wagatha Christie' ... 361. Someone's photoshopped your face and Mrs Vardy's face on to something from Scooby Doo? Unmasking a villain... these images were saved on your phone?

COLEEN. Yes.

TOMLINSON. ... And on page 364 there is, someone has put your face on to the cover of an Agatha Christie book.

COLEEN. Yes.

TOMLINSON. You saved that?

COLEEN. Yes.

TOMLINSON. You were delighted by the reaction that you received, weren't you?

COLEEN. No, I wasn't. I have never craved press attention in my life.

TOMLINSON. Mrs Rooney, this isn't a criticism, but you've used your fame for commercial purposes, you've had columns, you have been on television, you've made Netflix documentaries, you have done all that kind of thing, haven't you?

COLEEN. Yes, I have been fortunate that I have had... things have come my way but I've took the opportunities and used them. I wanted to continue on at school... but the pressure became quite big at a young age. And I was getting opportunities, which is why Paul Stretford... he took things on. And I felt like that was something that I could then control, in a way... I think I've done alright and obviously I haven't worked for a while because I've had children, I just wanted to be a mum. But I've never dwelled in the public eye. I have never asked for it. I was threw into it and I've worked with it.

TOMLINSON. ... It must have been obvious to you that putting this up was going to lead to Mrs Vardy being abused, wasn't it?

COLEEN. No that wasn't my intention at all. Not at all. I would not ever – it's not in my nature to cause abuse or trolling in any way at all.

TOMLINSON. ... You knew that... Mrs Vardy was receiving vitriol and abuse, didn't you?

COLEEN. I know, and it's disgusting.

TOMLINSON. ... And you attacked her in the [reveal] post, didn't you?

COLEEN. No... I haven't attacked her... you know, I have called her out and said this is who I believe whose account it is. I've not used vicious words... I could have done it a lot worse than that, you know, what – I thought that was an okay way of putting it really.

TOMLINSON. So when she was abused, what did you do to put it right?

COLEEN. ... Mrs Vardy directed lawyers on the day I put it out, so it was in their hands from that day on... I've never been in a court, I've never been in a legal case before... this is the first time publicly I have ever spoke about this... I have gone under instruction of my legal team.

TOMLINSON. So you're saying that you wanted to mitigate the abuse but your legal team advised you not to?

COLEEN. ... No, I've been silent. I didn't want to be in this court today. I didn't want to be here. I don't want to be here. But obviously Mrs Vardy has brought me here... I've put up with it for years and years – that – the stories that get wrote. This was different. It was a group of people I had accepted into my personal space and they were then going on to a national newspapers, which goes out to millions, and giving my information without consent.

TOMLINSON. And you know that your case over the past two and a half years has been conducted in a way that Mrs Vardy has... been accused of deliberately destroying documents, contempt of court... and cynically betraying her own friend [Caroline Watt].

COLEEN. ... Yes.

TOMLINSON. ... The truth is this, Mrs Rooney... you do not actually have any evidence to link Mrs Vardy to the leaking of material from your private Instagram.

COLEEN. ... I believe that it was Mrs Vardy.

TOMLINSON. ...There isn't a shred of evidence... is there? You just think that she's the kind of person that leaks... is that your case?

COLEEN. ... I believe all the evidence I have points the finger that Mrs Vardy knew exactly what was going on.

TOMLINSON. ... Thank you. No further questions.

STEYN. Thank you. Mr Sherborne.

> (**MR TOMLINSON** *sits*. **MR SHERBORNE** *stands.*)

SHERBORNE. ... Quickly, Mrs Rooney. You were asked by Mr Tomlinson why you didn't do anything after the reveal post.... There was a threatening letter [from Mrs

Vardy's legal team] ....can I take you back to bundle C... p411... This is written to you personally, isn't it?

COLEEN. Yes.

SHERBORNE. ... You can see it says... "Please also ensure that all material pertaining to this matter has been preserved. This includes all versions of the post... Under no circumstances must the Twitter post and Instagram post be deleted"

COLEEN. ... Yes. This is why I haven't touched the posts.

SHERBORNE. ... No further questions, thank you, Mrs Rooney.

(**COLEEN** *sits. The* **PUNDITS** *gather.*)

PUNDIT 2. Unbelievable, Jeff. Vendettas, missing messages – and, like Tomlinson just said, not a shred of evidence.

PUNDIT 1. I'm not sure about that. Sherborne proved that Rebekah had a relationship with *The Sun*, he proved that she's sold stories on other people –

PUNDIT 2. Proved is a matter of opinion –

PUNDIT 1. And Coleen has screenshots of the fake Instagram posts, which clearly say 'seen by one'. Rebekah Vardy's account. What more do you want?

PUNDIT 2. But that doesn't necessarily mean *The Sun* stories came directly from Rebekah. She could have innocently screenshot the gender selection post and sent it to a friend, who then sent it on to *The Sun* without her knowledge. Or she could have mentioned it in passing at a party, to someone who then went and told *The Sun*.

PUNDIT 1. I think that's a stretch, Jem. And in court, there were other witnesses who gave evidence for Coleen ... Rachel Monk, Coleen's PR. Joe Mcloughlin, Coleen's brother and social media manager. They were called to back up Coleen's evidence that neither knew of her Vardy-catching plan. Oh, and how could I forget – Harpreet Robertson, Rebekah Vardy's favourite FA official. She was called to discuss the seat mix-up at the Euros.... and we should – yeah, we do – have a clip from Harpreet on the stand here –

HARPREET. "Becky's evidence on this topic is simply untrue".

PUNDIT 1. Thank you, Harpreet.

PUNDIT 2. After Wayne Rooney's helpful testimony –

WAYNE ROONEY. This.. has been the first time of me really having any understanding of how it's all happened.

PUNDIT 2. Both teams called tech experts to the stand. For Coleen Rooney, this was Matthew Blackbland. He did say that it was highly probable that Rebekah's WhatsApp files were manually deleted, but you know, he was Coleen's witness, so –

PUNDIT 1. Yeah, but subbed in for Rebekah Vardy's team was tech expert Ian Rutherford. He didn't go quite as far as that, but he did say the disappearance of her messages was 'somewhat surprising'. And that's *her own* witness.

PUNDIT 2. We also heard from Claire Rooney, Paul Stretford, and an independent witness Penelope Adaarewa.

PUNDIT 1. All of them were Coleen Rooney's witnesses. No other witnesses for Rebekah Vardy came to court.

PUNDIT 2. Except outside the court, there was one quiet, supportive voice, who had listened to Wayne's testimony with quiet rage. Jamie Vardy. He issued a statement via his legal team –

(**PUNDIT 1** *becomes* **JAMIE VARDY.**)

JAMIE VARDY. Wayne is talking nonsense. He must be confused because he never spoke to me about issues concerning Becky's media work at Euro 2016. There was nothing to speak about. I know this because I discuss everything with Becky.

PUNDIT 2. We're on day seven now. The final day of court, and an entire day of closing statements from Tomlinson and Sherborne.

PUNDIT 1. This is the final chance for our lawyers to lay out their case. And if Sherborne hasn't won on the truth defence – which I reckon he has – he'll argue that Coleen's reveal post was published in the public interest.

PUNDIT 2. Which is ridiculous, I mean this was an online spat between frenemies.

PUNDIT 1. Rebekah Vardy set herself up as a public figure, Jem. She did TV work, columns, she sold things to us. She even fronted campaigns about how to behave properly online.

PUNDIT 2. Having an Instagram account doesn't make you a public figure.

PUNDIT 1. It does if you're using it to build a career. Rebekah was monetising public trust. And it's in our interest to know if we can trust her or not.

PUNDIT 2. I think that's for our Judge to decide.

(The barristers rise.)

PUNDIT 2. On the 'truth defence', Tomlinson argued that Rebekah was unjustly defamed by Coleen Rooney's post –

TOMLINSON. … The allegation in the post was false… [And] as a result of the post, Mrs Vardy and her family were subjected to abuse and threats of a really horrific nature –

PUNDIT 2. He also argued that there were many WhatsApp messages between Caroline Watt and Rebekah Vardy which actually speak to their innocence. For example, on 6th February, when Coleen first unfollowed Rebekah, she writes to Caroline –

REBEKAH. "She thinks it's me that's been doing stories on her! Of all the people on her Instagram FFS".

SHERBORNE. ... 'FFS'. What does FFS stand for?

REBEKAH. I'm –

STEYN. It is fine.

REBEKAH. Is it OK?

STEYN. Yes.

REBEKAH. For Fucks Sake...

PUNDIT 1. In his closing statement, Sherborne argued that his team had *proved* the truth defence. He believed he'd demonstrated that Rebekah Vardy was responsible for leaking Coleen Rooney's private stories –

SHERBORNE. This is a detective story and like any good detective story you never find the person responsible standing over the body with a smoking gun in her hand... if [Mrs Vardy] gave Ms [Caroline] Watt the gun and the bullets, told her who to target, knew where it was happening and gave her blessing... it makes her just as responsible as the person who pulled the trigger.

PUNDIT 1. He also argued the strong possibility that Rebekah was party to destroying evidence.

SHERBORNE. ... RIP Ms Watt's phone.

PUNDIT 2. Finally, on the much contested public interest defence. Tomlinson told us once again that this was just gossip. A private social media saga, comprising mostly of information that Coleen actually *wanted* Rebekah to leak to the press.

TOMLINSON. This is a quintessentially private matter... A falling out between two individuals... there is no doubt that this is of great interest to the public, but the information that Mrs Rooney was concerned about as deriving from her private Instagram was... low value tittle tattle.

PUNDIT 1. But privacy is subjective, Jem.

SHERBORNE. Just because [it wasn't] about some government act or some crimes committed by a well-known figure or celebrity, doesn't mean it doesn't come within the wide ambit of public interest in this modern age, where social media is the vast majority of people's everyday life and communication.

PUNDIT 2. Closing his case, Tomlinson asked for substantial damages, based on the emotional toll this has taken on his client.

TOMLINSON. ... Someone on social media called her an 'evil rat-faced bitch' and said she should go on to die and that her baby deserved to be put in an incinerator.

PUNDIT 1. While Sherborne asked for the case to be immediately dismissed –

SHERBORNE. ... Mrs Vardy brings this case after two years and hundreds of thousands of pounds being spent. I do wonder whether it is not just Mrs Rooney but this whole court that may well think now, why on earth are we here?

PUNDIT 1. And still... neither could agree on the role of our mystery PR.

(**PUNDIT 2** *becomes* **CAROLINE**.)

(*The others circle her. She listens.*)

Was Caroline Watt the villain of this piece? Or was she was just a good PR doing her job. Getting her client, Rebekah Vardy, positive press in exchange for stories about other people in Rebekah's world? A game that most people in their industry play.

TOMLINSON. ... Mrs Vardy is reluctant... to accuse Caroline Watt... of doing something wrong but she sees, as everybody else does, the indications point that way.

PUNDIT 1. There's one thing we do know, though. Caroline isn't a public figure. She was just a private citizen, caught in the crossfire of two women at war.

SHERBORNE. ... Mrs Vardy...feels she has been betrayed [by Caroline Watt]. We say that's a lie.

PUNDIT 1. Of course, Caroline wasn't there to defend herself –

SHERBORNE. ... No Caroline Watt [in this court] is like Hamlet without the Prince of Denmark.

PUNDIT 1. And finally, as the game came to a close, our Judge was left to deliberate.

> (**STEYN** *blows the whistle and the game is over.*)

> (*The court disbands.*)

> (*Until –.*)

Until the 29th July 2022 . And we're here today, with Mrs Justice Steyn, ready to deliver her verdict. The atmosphere is electric, we've got two teams facing each other again after –

> (**PUNDIT 1** *touches his earpiece.*)

Oh – right – erm, sorry. The verdict was actually posted online.

> (*The broadcast is over.*)

> (*Around the* **PUNDIT**, *the court dismantles.*)

(Barristers leave. Only **REBEKAH**, **COLEEN** *and* **CAROLINE** *remain.)*

There was nobody actually in court. There were no filled stadiums. No moonboots, no costumes. Maybe Coleen was in the car when she found out. Maybe she was at home. Maybe Rebekah saw the buzz of a message from her lawyer, and her heart raced. Maybe Caroline switched her phone off. Maybe she hid herself away. But wherever they were, without fanfare, our Judge published her verdict...

*(***COLEEN**, **REBEKAH** *and* **CAROLINE** *sit separately.)*

(Their phones buzz with the Judge's verdict.)

(As they read, we're on **STEYN**.)*

STEYN. This judgement is given following a seven day trial of this libel claim which is brought by the claimant, Ms Rebekah Vardy, against the defendant, Ms Coleen Rooney.

... It was evident that Ms Vardy found the process of giving evidence stressful and, at times, distressing. I bear in mind when assessing her evidence the degree of stress she was naturally feeling, given the high profile nature of the trial, the abuse that she has suffered since the reveal post was published, and the length of time she was in the witness box.

... I find that it is, unfortunately, necessary to treat Mrs Vardy's evidence with very considerable caution. There were many occasions when her evidence was manifestly inconsistent with the contemporaneous documentary evidence... Mrs Vardy was generally unwilling to make factual concessions, however implausible her evidence.

... I have found that Mrs Vardy was party to the disclosure to *The Sun* of the Marriage, Birthday,

Halloween, Pyjamas, Car Crash, Gender Selection, Babysitting and Flooded Basement Posts... It is likely that Ms Watt undertook the direct act [of passing information] on to a journalist at *The Sun*. In my view, Mrs Vardy knew of and condoned this behaviour, actively... directing Ms Watt to the private Instagram account [and] sending her screenshots of Mrs Rooney's posts.

I will express my decision in respect of the public interest defence very briefly... although Mrs Rooney's interest was essentially personal, on balance, I accept that the reveal post was on a matter of public interest... I accept that Mrs Rooney believed, having given several warnings on her private Instagram account, as well as a public warning, that it was in the public interest to publish the reveal post.

... For the reasons I have given, the claim is dismissed.

> (**COLEEN** *and* **REBEKAH** *look up from their phones – both with a hint of a smile.)*
>
> *(Sunglasses on, they leave the stage.)*
>
> *(But we're left with* **CAROLINE**. *Alone, before –.)*
>
> *(Blackout.)*

ABOUT THE AUTHOR

Liv Hennessy is a screen and theatre writer from the West Midlands. In 2020, she was a finalist in the Paines Plough Women's Prize for Playwriting with her debut play *Colostrum*. In 2022, Liv was one of the writers selected for the BBC TV Pilot Scheme. Previously, she has worked as Story Producer and Story Editor on ITV's *Emmerdale*.

Ingram Content Group UK Ltd.
Milton Keynes UK
UKHW021837280423
420952UK00011B/233

9 780573 013652